MY ANGER MY CHILD

Strategies For Anger Management, Staying Calm And Maintaining a Calm Environment

Richie R. Radford

TABLE OF CONTENTS

PART 1: MY ANGER

CHAPTER 1: WHAT DOES ANGER MEAN AS A PARENT?

People experience anger naturally. Anger may occasionally be good. For instance, anger may give you the drive you need to complete a task or stand up for what you believe in.

Setting a good example for your children can also be accomplished by feeling furious and controlling such emotions positively and healthily. You can teach your kids how to act by taking a few calm breaths or choosing to leave rather than shouting, for instance. However, anger can be harmful, particularly if it occurs frequently or spirals out of control.

Getting furious and losing your temper might exacerbate issues and cause you to clash with other people. If you don't allow yourself to relax, you might say or act in a harmful or unhelpful manner.

Also, because children need to feel safe and comfortable to grow and develop, it is unhealthy for them to be around a lot of conflicts and yelling.
We believe we need to defend ourselves from a threat when we are angry. We fail to recognize that a misbehaving child is simply a youngster who is confused or disturbed and has an immature intellect, not a danger. We fail to realize that when we act threateningly ourselves, we are adding to the drama.

We neglect the fact that it is our duty as parents to conduct ourselves maturely while calmly guiding our children so they can learn, mature, and gain the capacity to control their own emotions and behavior.
You'll know your child is the issue when their behavior causes you to lose it and throw a fit. However, when you "lose it," it means you've been triggered.

WHY DO I GET ANGRY AT MY KIDS

For a variety of reasons, parents may get angry around their kids. Parents may have a lot on their plates, such as caring for family members, working, maintaining the household's finances, doing chores, and running errands. They could feel worried or overburdened as a result, which makes it easier for them to lose patience and get furious.

Children may act harshly toward a parent or other people, refuse to cooperate, or do what a parent requests. These actions might make a parent angry. Due to a partner or other adult living in the home, a parent could become angry. People may dispute, for instance, on matters such as discipline, parenting methods, or domestic duties.

People may also feel dissatisfied or furious if they have additional constraints on them, such as stress connected to their job, sleeplessness, weariness, medical or mental disease, or money problems. These concerns can make it tougher to be patient and calm when responding to the demands of a child.

People may also feel postnatal anger after giving birth, which may be related to a range of variables such as shifting hormones, sleep deprivation, and the stress of parenthood.

Your child may be pushing your buttons, but he isn't triggering your response. Any situation that makes you feel like lashing out has roots in your own early years. We know this because we lose our capacity to think rationally at those moments, and we start acting like kids ourselves, throwing our own tantrums.

Don't worry. That's normal. We all approach the parenting process wounded in some manner from our childhoods, and our kids reveal all those scars. We might anticipate our kids to behave out in ways that throw us over the edge at times. That's why it's our obligation as the grownup to keep away from the edge.

MISCONCEPTIONS ABOUT PARENTING

Parenting tips are abounding. It can seem like there's a new trend every week boasting about the finest way to raise your kids or warning about the worst. With so many prescriptions for excellent parenting, understandably, it may rapidly grow complicated and frustrating. Below are the most prevalent myths and misconceptions regarding parenting revealed by two psychologists.

Myth 1: If your kids aren't happy, something is very wrong.

In our culture, there's a tremendous emphasis on happiness, so if your kids aren't happy most of the time or in particular situations, parents start to worry. But it's normal and good for kids to feel lots of highs and lows, said Jessica Michaelson, PsyD, a clinical psychologist and founder of Honest Parenthood, who specializes in early parent-child relationships.

This “is considerably richer and authentic than a monochromatic ‘happy’ life.”

According to Michaelson, each of us is born with a range of emotional experiences, some having more negative feelings than others. It’s healthy to be “able to feel and deal with all of them.”

For example, Parents are throwing a birthday celebration for their child. They anticipate her to be cheerful and excited. But the child becomes anxious in groups and new situations and argues with a classmate.

"She may be delighted that there's a celebration with all her pals and tasty cake, etc., but is furious about being overstimulated, afraid by the loud noises, and nervous about the preschool classmate," Michaelson said.

(She highlighted that chronic dissatisfaction may be troublesome.

It may be a symptom that your child is battling with depression. Some kids with depression may scream and have low energy and disrupted sleep. Others may be irritable, anxious, and confrontational, she said. The key is to see these signs consistently. "Of sure, suicidal gestures and ideas are red flags.")

Myth 2: Parents shouldn't tell their kids no.

This is a new trend Maui clinical psychologist Heather Wittenberg, Psy.D, has been witnessing. The reason? "The prior generations of American parents were more strict out of need as it was just a more tough time, but the kids grew up to feel unfairly judged, as a group."

Today, the pendulum has swung the opposite way, she said. Now it's felt that saying no to kids is too harsh and perhaps detrimental.

However, putting limitations teaches kids numerous skills and helps them to feel protected, said Wittenberg, also the author of Let's Get This Potty Started! Saying no "doesn't hurt and is good, as long as it's not said in an aggressive or antagonistic tone. The context is considerably more important than the actual word."

Other instances of useful boundary setting include suspending your teen's cell phone access because they went over their minutes (and having them earn additional money to get the phone back); and removing your toddler from a party until he can calm down and express his frustrations in words.

Myth 3: Good parenting is about good strategies.

"It is incredibly enticing to limit successful parenting to a set of specific methods and processes, but it doesn't work like that," Michaelson said.

Instead of a particular parenting style, what's more important, she said, is the parents' mindset: how they think, feel and interact with the environment.
It revealed that a mother's attachment style "her ability to trust, her expectations of relationships, and how she connects to her feelings" during pregnancy predicted the child's attachment style at 12 months.
"We can forecast how secure a child is going to be based on how secure the mother feels before even having the baby."
Self-confident parents tend to raise self-confident kids, Michaelson added. Parents who have healthy connections tend to have kids who have healthy relationships. Parents who believe in work leading to positive results and tenacity after failure are likely to create kids who are resilient and hopeful, she said.

In contrast, "parents who predict the worst tend to caution their children and encourage concern and self-doubt."

Because they prefer to shun problems, she added, these parents deter their kids from taking risks and meddling in their activities so they don't fail.

Michaelson works with parents who are frightened to do what seems right to them because an expert warned against it. Take the example of time-outs. There's another trend that timeouts are psychologically destructive since they cause kids to feel abandoned, shamed, and overwhelmed, she said.

Her clientele who've used timeouts quit utilizing them. That's when "things came apart at home."

"Many parents can utilize this tool politely and compassionately, and many children feel restrained and supported with this kind of tangible restriction and break from stimulation."

Michaelson believes that a better method is for parents to uncover their parenting instincts and experiment with what works best for their specific child.

She defined proper parenting as being aware and receptive to your child's needs. This involves being present and engaged, and acting in the moment, she said.

Myth 4: Good parents put their kids' needs first.

"Children may be all-consuming, and our culture can promote a very child-obsessed way of life," Michaelson added. This leaves many parents ignoring their personal needs, she added.

But it's crucial for parents to "put their oxygen masks on first," Wittenberg said. This not only helps you stay healthy, but it also conveys to your kids that parents are at the top of the family system, she said.

They “are there so that they can safeguard the little ones from harm. When children are in charge, deep down they feel scared because they know this upsets the system that was meant to protect them.”

Myth 5: Your marriage will survive neglect, while you're raising the kids.

Again, because parenting is all-consuming, some parents also neglect their marriages. "The early years of parenthood can easily drive partners apart from one another, and many many couples do not survive this neglect," Michaelson said.

For instance, couples might only communicate when there's conflict, engage in individual activities, and not spend time without their kids. The marriage becomes one-dimensional, she said, focused solely on parenting, not friendship or intimacy.

"Since our children learn how to have close relationships by watching us do it, one of the most important things we can do for our children is nurturing our connection with our partners," Michaelson said.

She suggested parents do this by thanking, complementing, and touching each other. "This lets each be a source of comfort and strength for each other during the everyday slog of parenting."

She also suggested having fun without the kids. Pick activities that involve laughter and something new such as learning to sail or activities you used to enjoy together, she said.

When it comes to parenting, there's a plethora of dos and don'ts. And this plethora tends to change regularly. Ultimately, it seems like the key to good parenting (and good life) is to remain engaged with yourself, your partner, and your kids.

SIGNS OF AN ANGRY PARENT

You can feel when you're starting to get angry – your body gives you signs. Those signs include:

Agitation, feeling annoyed, tense, or grumpy Those signs include:

- tense or clenching – shoulders, jaw, and hands, for example
- heart racing
- churning stomach
- faster breathing

You can also find yourself having unpleasant thoughts. Say you've had a long day at work, and you're going to have to work tonight to get on top of everything that has to be done. You pick your child up from daycare and they're grumpy, and start to grizzle and cry when you put them in the car. You get home and instruct them to go and wash their hands, and they sit on the ground and have a tantrum. This makes you feel frustrated and angry. You might be thinking 'If you'd just cooperated, I wouldn't be so angry!' 'You're so naughty why can't you just do what I ask for once!'

If you can recognize these signs of anger, you need to stop and do something to calm down, or you're likely to lose your temper and explode with anger.

CHAPTER 2: IDENTIFYING AND TACKLING MY TRIGGERS AS A PARENT

The key to discovering your triggers is to pay attention to your sensations and look for patterns in your reactions.

7 TRIGGER CLUES!

1. Any time you find yourself extremely upset at the kids (you know – the yelling at the top of your lungs, sweaty palms, red-faced, vein-popping sort) you've been triggered!
2. Any time you feel truly sad, disturbed, or hurt after your child did or said something, but you know you shouldn't take it personally — you've been triggered.
3. If the unhappy, afraid, or furious sensations are out of proportion to the circumstances (which you understand when you cool down) - you've probably been triggered.

4. If you feel like your reactions are out of your control, you've definitely been triggered.
5. If you feel like you've experienced this kind of feeling many times before and it feels quite familiar, you've been triggered.
6. If the feelings seem to come out of nowhere (calm to hair-pulling-out anger in 0 to 2 seconds flat!), you've been triggered.
7. If you find yourself immediately wanting to grab, slap, spank or otherwise physically damage your child, you've obviously been triggered.

TACKLING MY TRIGGERS AS A PARENT

You likely know what phrases or behaviors can trigger your sentiments fast. All of us are subject to the deep emotions that can readily erupt when someone pushes our buttons. When many of us reach our tipping point, we have to face the hardships and disappointments of parenting our children which frequently makes us address our fears and unhealed emotions. When youngsters do not listen, you could sense you are being overlooked. Parenting frequently exposes our darker, deep nature often buried away from public view. When we lash back, explode or unleash our emotions on our children we often feel hopeless and guilty from our lack of self-control. This can be a vicious cycle.

ACKNOWLEDGING UNHEALED EMOTIONS

The key strategy to taking control of your triggers and buttons is to notice, recognize and calm the unhealed feelings that keep you from managing yourself. It is crucial to know that when the emotional side of your brain takes control, you tend to react to situations by screaming and yelling.

However, you might also shut down, ignore the problem, withdraw yourself from the situation or turn a blind eye to any unpleasant behavior. Usually, your triggers are based on some feelings that could include:

- Guilt
- Fear
- Inadequacy
- Helplessness
- Hopelessness

Once you learn to know your buttons and triggers, you can pick a different reaction to your children's behavior.

In addition to your triggers, take attention if your throat begins to stiffen and your shoulders become tense. If your remarks are defensive or nasty, your buttons are certainly being pushed.

ALTER YOUR FEELINGS

Write down your sentiments to attempt to understand yourself and why certain acts make you upset. Are you feeling powerless, unsure, terrified, overwhelmed, or out of control? Are your feelings rational or irrational? Is there something you can do to influence your feelings?

It is crucial to realize what is at stake when you respond badly. Because you are the adult in the room, it is your obligation to provide positive influence when dealing with your child's negative behavior. If you take time to heal your wounds, you can avoid common power battles and begin to reestablish family unity through peaceful parenting.

POPULAR ANGER TRIGGERS IN PARENTING

We all have horrible days as parents, sometimes bad weeks and months. Parenting may be an emotionally draining path with long days and sleepless nights, believe me, I know.

But if you find that you've been experiencing more days than not when you are yelling at the kids or resorting to endless time-outs or even spankings, Then I hope you stick to reading as the knowledge I'm going to provide might just transform the scenario

When you learn about these parenting triggers, it may make such a massively good effect on your own life, and your parenting approach.

COMMON PARENTING TRIGGERS

If we want to be able to respond to our kids in the most positive, effective ways, then we need to become aware of our triggers.
SOME OF THE MOST COMMON PARENTING TRIGGERS ARE:

- Crying
- Whining
- Tantrums

A child disobeying, being non-compliant, or passively resistant
Siblings fighting. Anything else that your child does that makes you feel suddenly and irrationally angry or upset!

PART 2: MY CHILD

CHAPTER 4: WHY DOES MY CHILD GET ANGRY

Explosive kids can blow up over everything and everything. It can be frustrating for parents who need to deal with rage issues in their kids. Let's discuss what causes anger difficulties in a child, and how to assist them to develop proper coping skills and healthy strategies to prevent overwhelming rage. In younger toddlers, high emotions and temper tantrums are frequent as they start learning how to moderate their big feelings and temper tantrums. It is tough to have an angry child at home. It can put considerable strain on the family. You never know what little thing would set them off and turn a normal activity into a storm of angry outbursts or physical destruction. It's frustrating and exhausting for parents and family members to deal with.

How did a sweet baby turn into a ball of rage?

Scientists have found that anger can appear in infants as young as 4 months old. Anger reactivity increases over time and peaks at around 18-21 months of age. This phase in toddlerhood is widely characterized as the "terrible twos". Many anger issues start developing during this period when the small child starts to become mobile and exploratory.

Humans are wired to be curious. Toddlers are motivated learners. They like to seek novelty and learn new abilities. When young children start walking and becoming mobile, they want to explore the world around them. However, their exploratory actions are typically met with prohibition, scolding, or even harsh punishment.

Frustrated toddlers do not have the emotion regulation skills to deal with them. They also have a hard time expressing themselves or arguing for their requirements.

Temper tantrum results as the child raises their expression of rage but still cannot have their demands met.

An angry toddler may start with grunting and growling but as their furious sentiments intensify, they progress to shouting, screaming, punching, and kicking. If the parent feels furious and starts scolding or disciplining, the child's extreme anger will become increasingly persistent leading to anger disorders.

What Exactly Makes Children Angry? A child's difficulty controlling their rage might be caused by two different types of circumstances. biological variables, such as genetics or diseases, and early-life environmental influences. Both can result in a child's inability to control their emotions.

BIOLOGICAL CAUSES OF ANGER IN CHILDREN

TEMPERAMENT

Genetically, certain children can be born with a more challenging temperament. They are easily upset and more "angry-prone" . Infants with such a temperament display increased physiological responsiveness (which they were less able to regulate), poorer attention, and higher activity levels.

HEREDITY

A study has discovered that if a birth mother has high levels of anger, her toddler is more likely to also have high levels of anger when they're exposed to hostile scenarios.

ENVIRONMENTAL CAUSES OF ANGER IN CHILDREN

PARENTING STYLE

In toddlers, studies have discovered that parents' regulating behavior is associated with the child's anger and externalizing behavior.

The child's noncompliance also predicts an increase in the parent's controlling conduct, establishing a coercive cycle.

PARENT'S EMOTIONAL REACTION

The parent's reaction to their child's anger matters. If the parent exhibits anger while the toddler is furious, the child tends to have persistent anger and noncompliant conduct.

CHILD MALTREATMENT, ABUSE, AND SHAME

Children who are maltreated with physical abuse or shame are more prone to have emotional difficulties during confrontations. If children are severely chastised, criticized, treated with hostile rejection, or ignored by their primary caregiver, they may believe that they are unwanted, unlovable, and "bad". These negative self-beliefs amplify the humiliation experienced in the day-to-day unfavorable interactions. When embarrassed, youngsters may try to avoid this profoundly negative, painful emotion by displacing shame with feelings of wrath.

MARITAL HOSTILITY

Family dynamics is another environmental aspect that might affect a child's ability to self-regulate. Parents' interactions among themselves and with other adults serve as relational role models.

Angry exchanges between parents, even when they're not directed at the child, influence how youngsters view relationships and their future interactions with others. Kids with angry or aggressive parents are more prone to demonstrate anger and aggressive conduct that interferes with their everyday existence.

ANGER MANAGEMENT FOR KIDS

Anger management for children should consist of two parts: dealing with anger in the moment and anger prevention.

ANGER MANAGEMENT IN THE MOMENT

When your child is raging, they are in a fight-or-flight mode and cannot regulate themselves. It is up to you to help your child calm down.

When a kid is emotionally dysregulated, the amygdala, the part of the brain that expresses emotions, is in charge while the prefrontal cortex, the part that can think logically, is offline. Therefore, you cannot and should not reason with an angry child.

Here are a few ways that can calm your child's nervous system.

ACKNOWLEDGING

Acknowledge their anger and name their emotions. You don't need to agree with or approve of their feelings. Simply describe it without adding any judgment or defending yourself.

"I can see that you are very angry. It feels so unfair."

They, and we all, want to be heard. Sometimes, acknowledging is all it takes to calm a storm.

SLOW DEEP BREATHS BOTH OF YOU

Taking steady deep breaths can soothe an excited nervous system. Teach your kid to slowly breathe in, count to five, and then breathe out, and do it with them to calm your own body.

HUGGING

Physical contact such as hugging can assist your child settle down quickly because it directly quiets your child's nervous system. If your child is raging, they may not want to be touched. In that scenario, stay with your child and use closeness to assist them in regulating. However, if your child is injuring himself or others, hugging can protect them in addition to comforting them.

DISTRACTION

Distraction may be employed when your youngster can still listen to you. Guide them to think of something enjoyable or cheerful, e.g. recent vacation to the beach, when they made a Lego airplane, holding a puppy, etc.

ANGER MANAGEMENT – PREVENTION

REDUCE INCIDENTS THAT CAN CAUSE FRUSTRATION

For young toddlers, shifting from one activity to another can easily generate rage and frustration. Give warnings to prepare your toddler or preschooler for changes.

It's easy to believe that anger in older kids is the result of them not obtaining what they want. But it's more than that.

“Anger is always directed on someone in particular, ... not toward all of humanity.”

Youngsters don't get furious all by themself. So anger problems can be considered relationship problems as anger only arises in the contact between parties.

As in any relationship, there are two sides to every story.

Grownups typically assume that youngsters are carefree and sad feelings are wrong.

- But think about what children experience every day. Here are several examples:
- You have to wake up when you're told to.
- You have to eat whatever breakfast is made for you.
- You have your activities during the day chosen for you.
- You have to sit in class for hours a day.
- You have to ask for permission to use the bathroom.
- You have to do your homework when you get home.
- You cannot go out without your parents' consent.
- You have to stop playing your favorite video game when the screen time is up.
- You cannot remain up late.
- You cannot reason with your parents because that's considered talking back

- You're given orders by grownups all the time.
- You are not always talked to respectfully but you cannot exhibit any disrespect in return.
- The list continues...

Will you be able to perform all of the above day after day, and if you refuse, you'll be nagged, chastised, or punished, without feeling angry?
The truth is, we, the parents, are often the source of our children's rage. We believe that a lot of things we ask our children to do are good for them and hence reasonable. And we assume we're always correct.
No one is always right.
To prevent rage produced by us, treat your youngster properly and with respect.

There's a difference between training our kids to do the right thing and forcing our kids to do what we want.

There’s also a difference between what is proper and what is desirable.
When we think we're correct, we need to explain to them the reasons. When we realize we're not right, we need to be open to change.
There’s a difference between training our kids to do the right thing and forcing our kids to do what we want. There’s also a difference between what is proper and what is desirable.
When we think we're correct, we need to explain the reasons. When we realize we're not right, we need to be open to change.

LOOK OUT FOR TIREDNESS AND HUNGER

Children, or anyone, are more prone to wrath when they are sleepy or hungry. Address those requirements, e.g. snacking or sleeping, obtaining enough sleep if those are the underlying reasons for rage.

PARENT IN A WARM, SENSITIVE, AND RESPONSIVE WAY

Plenty of studies have indicated that parents' sensitive reactions which promote secure attachment in the child are protective for youngsters who are anger-prone.

Securely bonded children have stronger self-control and self-esteem. They tend to moderate and express anger in socially useful ways.

CHAPTER 5: HOW MY ANGER AFFECTS MY CHILD

Parental rage can have serious impacts on children. Children may blame themselves if a parent is furious. And parental anger may cause a child to feel anxious, which can alter how their brain grows. Growing up around rage is a risk factor for mental illness in later life.

Parental rage may result in emotional or verbal abuse toward a child. If a parent speaks harmful words to a child out of anger, the child may assume it is their fault and develop feelings of worthlessness.

Children may respond to upset parents with poor conduct, rudeness, or hostility. Children may also become unwell, withdraw from others, or have difficulties sleeping.

If rage evolves into physical aggression, it might badly hurt a child. Shaking, striking, or throwing a newborn could cause severe injury, incapacity, or death.

Punishing a child physically can also negatively influence them later in life, possibly leading in:

- antisocial behavior
- aggression
- poor self-esteem
- mental health issues
- negative associations

CHAPTER 6: STRATEGIES FOR BETTER PARENTING

Parents need help and encouragement in this crucial job. When parents realize where they are and where their child is at, they may be more intentional in the ways they parent. The goal is to find areas they haven't been aware of as parents and to make changes if needed. Taking the time and being kind to themselves and becoming conscious of how they parent is the first step.

Here are some crucial approaches to meeting those daily parenting problems.

BREATHE

Instead of reacting in fury, offering a quick punishment, or casting blame on the child, practicing conscious parenting can look like taking a few seconds to breathe and be calm.

REFLECT

Parents must take time to think about whatever triggers or feelings an incident may have stirred inside them before expressing these emotions toward their child.

SET BOUNDARIES

Conscious parenting does require setting limits particularly when it comes to requesting respectful dialogue.

Make sure the youngster knows, and it may take a little while, but being constant is the best approach to teach them.

ACCEPT

Finally, instead of getting offended, accept what has happened and go on. Carrying whatever conduct or scenario has happened for the rest of the day, would only weaken the connection.

Taking time to reconnect is a vital last step.

Ways to do this include:

- explaining to a child that they are beginning to feel angry and need to step away for a few minutes to calm down

- focusing on taking long, deep breaths in and breathing out with a sigh, and repeating this until feeling calmer
- counting to 10 slowly, and repeating this until feeling calmer

If a person is able to put their child somewhere safe, they may be able to remove themselves from the situation for longer to calm down. They could try:

- taking a warm shower to calm the body
- walking outside to obtain some fresh air
- meditating or practicing mindfulness or deep breathing
- finding a quiet location to be alone

- exercising or doing physical exercise, such as going for a run, gardening, cleaning, or doing a house project
- doing an activity that they find relaxing, such as painting, listening to music, or reading a book or magazine

Once people feel calm, it might then be good to reflect on the situation.

People may be able to understand what provoked their anger and whether there is a solution to the problem or a means to live with it positively in the future. Certain strategies may work better for some people than others. People may wish to test multiple tactics to determine what works best for them and what conditions usually trigger them.

HOW TO COMMUNICATE YOUR WORDS WITHOUT YELLING

It’s normal to feel like you want to raise your voice during a tense conversation but there are dozens of methods, other than shouting, to attract your child’s attention. Learning to model calm conduct will help you and your child bond.

Yelling, losing your calm, raising your voice.... Pretty nearly everyone ends up doing it at some time. But try to remember that your kids will learn how to have effective dialogues by observing you. During tough talks with kids, it's crucial to be courteous and to demand respect in return. Here's how to make your point and promote good communication skills.

1. Take the opposing tone

Shouting "Stop yelling at me!" when you're arguing is unlikely to make anybody feel calmer. Model the sort of discussion skills you want your child to master. Try this: The louder your youngster becomes, the softer the tone you use to answer. This indicates that raising your voice isn't the method to solve problems. And it can make you both feel calmer. If your child has problems with social indicators like voice pitch and tone, you can point out later how your gentler approach helped.

2. Be a broken record

Sometimes there's no place for bargaining on an issue. In these instances, employ a cool, all-business tone and softly restate what you anticipate from your youngster. "Sorry, but when you hit, you sit." No of the reply you get, simply quietly repeat the same statement as many times as it takes.

Eventually, your message will sink in. This may be especially beneficial for youngsters who have problems remembering or paying attention to rules.

3. Ask questions

When there is potential for bargaining, some sentences may convert an argument into a healthy, back-and-forth conversation:
"What if you had 20 minutes of iPad time before homework?"
"Could we attempt to... " or "Would you be ready to give this a go for a week and then see whether it's working?"
"I wonder what you think is the greatest time to do your schoolwork each day." Using these brief, short words are particularly useful for youngsters who have receptive language problems or trouble focusing.

4. Be optimistic and clear

Being open and direct about what you want is vital. So is utilizing your child's name while providing directions. This will capture your child's attention and make your message more personal. This might be especially useful for youngsters with listening comprehension challenges. Instead of snapping, "The Xbox belongs to the whole family!" try stating, "Tommy, I'd want you to give your brother a turn now." using your natural tone as opposed to shouting your commands.

5. Make it fun

Defuse the heat with some levity. Instead of scolding distracted (or hyperactive) toddlers to sit still so they can clean their teeth, try some gentle and playful prodding. "Quick, Nathan, I see Elmo in your mouth and I need to brush him out. Oh, and Cookie Monster, too!"

Or, "You may choose a TV show every night this week if I don't have to remind you to tidy up your toys."

6. Take a rest

If you feel that one of you is going to lose control, call a time-out and take a big breath. Try stating something like, “Let’s both calm down. In 30 minutes, we can see if we’re ready to discuss again.” Then each of you may wander off to various rooms, cool off, and self-reflect. Keep in mind that “self-reflection” might be a challenging ability for a youngster who learns and thinks differently. But watching you model the conduct will assist. If you’re in a public area, remind your youngster that the conversation is on stop until you get in the car or make it home.

7. Control the conversation

When a topic is ready to go off the rails, it's crucial to halt it in its tracks. Unlike most youngsters, you have the grown-up self-awareness to pause and think: "Is what I'm about to say going to help or damage this situation? What about how I'm about to express it?" You have more self-control and better communication skills than you can expect a youngster to have. You have the power to disconnect, refocus, or restart the conversation more positively and beneficially.

8. Talk to others

Parenting a child who learns and thinks differently poses unique challenges. It might assist to become connected to other parents who've "been there, done that". They may be able to provide thoughts and comments based on their own experiences.

And just having someone who knows what you're going through might help you keep cool while an argument with your child is building.

CHAPTER 7: DEVELOPING A CALM HABIT

One of the first stages to regulating anger might be recognizing the indicators of rage. These can include:

- feeling irritated, annoyed, irritable, or tense
- tensing or clenching muscles, such as those in the jaw, shoulders, or hands
- a racing heart
- a churning or tight stomach
- breathing faster
- sweating
- having negative thoughts

Once people realize the indications of anger, they may take efforts to calm down and prevent themselves from communicating their wrath to their children.

All parents become irritated with their children. There's nothing wrong with experiencing rage; anger is a message. The difficulty is that we can't hear that message clearly when we're furious. In the heat of the moment, we're in a fight, flight, or freeze. And while we're in "battle," our child seems like the enemy. So we assume the message is that we should overcome the enemy — our child!

In reality, the message when your child becomes upset is that he needs your support, even if he's being impossible. (Especially when he's being impossible!)

Maybe we need to send him to bed an hour earlier or engage with him more, or simply make it safe enough for him to weep and show us all those emotions and worries that are making him act out. But we can't grasp or act on that message when we're prompted by our fear and fury. Staying calm is vital to fixing the situation, instead of making it worse.

So how can you keep calm when your youngster acts up, instead of drifting into the dark side?

1. Notice that you're growing upset.

Sometimes, we don't realize until we're already on the dark side. But normally we can see our annoyance increasing since we start accumulating kindling. What do I mean? We start examining all the reasons we're correct and our child is an ungrateful brat. Once you start accumulating kindling, it's hard to avoid the firestorm. So as soon as you recognize that your mental chatter regarding your child is negative, STOP. Drop your agenda (Just briefly) (Just temporarily.) Take a deep breath to stop the runaway locomotive of your rage.

2. Use your inner pause button.

Even if you're already well down the wrong path and you're ranting, STOP. Take a deep breath and push the pause button. Close your mouth, even in mid-sentence.

Don’t feel ashamed; you’re demonstrating effective anger control. Save your shame for when you have a tantrum.

3. Take Five.

Don't try to handle the matter with your child while you're furious. Calm down and become re-centered so you can genuinely hear the message underlying your rage. Are you scared about your child's behavior? Resentful against your partner? Exhausted and stressed out so you're overreacting to your child's regular age-appropriate behavior?

4. Feel the feelings in your body.

I'm not advocating that you swallow your anger, simply that you resist acting on it. Instead, sense the fury in your body. Really feel that pressure in your belly, that choking feeling in your throat. Breathe into those tight spots. As you are just open to the

sensations in your body, you'll feel them beginning to shift and dissolve.
That's the magic of mindfulness whenever we stay with those feelings, just accepting them with compassion, they fade away.

5. Shift your state.

Now, rephrase your thinking about the circumstance to produce other sentiments. If you're thinking that your youngster needs to be taught a significant lesson right now, you'll be angry. If you remind yourself that she's acting like a kid because she is a child and that she needs your love most when she seems to deserve it least, you'll be willing to shift out of anger.

6. Try a Do-Over.

Tell your youngster that you're sorry you got so upset, and the two of you are going to attempt a Do-over. This time, keep calm. Empathize.

Listen to your child's feelings and attempt to see things from her perspective. Resist the desire to blame, and instead search for solutions that work for both of you. If your child has harmed something including a relationship ask her what she might do to fix it. But always start by listening to her unhappiness and empathizing.

7. Practice, Practice, Practice.

I'm not going to lie to you. This is an incredibly hard job, one of the hardest things someone can undertake. If you're used to flying off the handle, you'll be training your brain with new patterns of self-discipline. That takes practice. Luckily, every time you avoid acting when you're furious, you're rewiring your brain, so regulating your anger gets simpler every time you do it.

Sure, you'll lose it occasionally. But if you simply keep practicing, holding yourself with compassion and noting the feelings, you'll discover that even when your child behaves up, you're better able to maintain calm. At some time, you'll notice that you rarely lose your anger anymore.

You'll still have juvenile conduct as long as you live among children, but your attitude will be different. A lot less drama, and a lot more love.

Yoda would be proud.

STRATEGIES FOR STAYING CALM

Everyone has a reaction to anger, but several tactics can assist in guaranteeing the anger does not become out of hand.

Strategies for controlling rage include:

- Recognizing the warning indicators. Being aware of the changes in the body, emotions, and behaviors that occur from anger can help someone determine how they want to react to a situation before they act.
- Pausing before responding. Walking away from the situation might afford

the person some time to ponder and take back control.

- Counting to 10. Taking a few seconds to count slowly to 10 helps diminish the intensity of the rage.
- Releasing stress in the body. To alleviate tension, unclench the jaw, lower the shoulders, and uncross the arms and legs. Roll the shoulders back and lengthen the neck to either side if retaining tension here.
- Listening. It might be tempting to leap to assumptions when irritated. If having a heated disagreement, take some time to stop and listen before reacting.
- Exercising. Doing cardiovascular workouts such as jogging, cycling, or swimming might assist release the energy that could otherwise become aggressiveness.

- Finding a distraction. Listening to music, dancing, going for a walk, writing in a notebook, or just taking a shower can all help prevent anger from increasing.

- Changing unfavorable mental habits. In the heat of the moment, the issue might appear much worse than it really is. An approach called cognitive restructuring can help people confront and replace hostile ideas.
- Using relaxation methods. Using relaxation practices, such as deep breathing and progressive muscle relaxation, may help decrease emotions of rage.

CHAPTER 8: MAINTAINING A CALM ENVIRONMENT

Children can hear and see numerous unpleasant, frequently scary pictures through television, newspapers, and the internet. As parents and caregivers of children, what can we do to create a serene atmosphere that children need?

Set the Emotional Tone

Think of how you feel entering a room of people. When you are greeted warmly, it portrays a pleasant mood; someone cares that you are there.

Apply this to your children by greeting them with a good morning with a grin! Adults caring for children may establish an emotional tone.

If adults are pleasant, compassionate, and attentive, the environment in the room will begin to reflect this.

Consider easy improvements to your household, such as displaying family photographs, class photos, and children's artwork/projects. Incorporate warm lighting and soft items (pillows, blankets, and comfy seats) (pillows, blankets, and comfortable chairs).

The surroundings should represent each family member and those things they find essential to them. During this time at home, assist your youngster to establish a particular spot to make their own. Help them make it personal and comfortable.

Family Time

Children need to feel a part of the family. Provide family moments together such as mealtimes, project times, and meeting times. It is in these times that youngsters are taught with a feeling of duty to care for one other and the environment.

Have the youngsters, together with the adults, develop rules or "living concepts" for the group. State and express the rules in a positive manner, such as "We use inside voices" vs. "No screaming." This is a crucial moment for both children and adults to share ideas, especially in addressing disagreements. Offering children "a voice" to talk and make decisions suggest that they are an important and capable member of the family.

Natural Connections

Nature has a way of providing beauty, a sense of peace, and creativity to any place.

Create chances daily to expose children to the outside world, especially getting outdoors to play! The fresh air and physical activity will give you a road to excellent health. Research reveals that children who are physically healthy are happy. Happier children create happier settings.

Display beautiful items from nature in the inside environment (especially those the children discovered!) such as seashells, leaves, flowers, rocks, interesting sticks, and plants.

The children begin to see the adult's respect and awe for natural materials and show a sense of honoring and caring for something. Caring for nature reflects caring for each other.

Engaging Environments

Lots of time and space to explore developmentally appropriate, fascinating, and creative stuff enables your children to focus. Boredom or having nothing to do might be the root of unpleasant behaviors, but a kid joyfully engrossed in play reflects an engaging environment and, in return, encourages a calm atmosphere.

Now is a wonderful time to rotate toys and activities, dig out some long-forgotten treasures, or enjoy previously outgrown hobbies like building blocks, or board games.

Be a Peaceful Role Model

Guiding and finding peaceful alternatives for children during a disagreement is one of the most essential skills that you can provide your children. Even at an early age, children may learn to start problem-solving and settling problems. Model words to encourage sharing and turn-taking:

- "You both want a turn playing on the iPad. How can you both get a turn?"
- "Your brother is listening to music. Did you want to ask him for a turn?"
- "How can we help each other?"

Role-playing is useful in practicing problem-solving. Offer the children age-appropriate tasks to solve such as, how should we organize the toy area. Practice different scenarios using puppets or tiny human miniatures to play out resolutions. Use regular experiences of sharing, clean-up, and being kind to reinforce positive examples with the kids.

Peaceful settings take time to establish and demand ongoing maintenance in order to sustain. In the process of establishing and implementing peaceful surroundings, we are, in turn, growing calm and loving children.

www.ingramcontent.com/pod-product-compliance
Lightning Source LLC
LaVergne TN
LVHW050340160826
845677LV00014B/3705